Letters to Colin Firth

Katherine Riegel

Sundress Publications
Knoxville, Tennessee, USA

ISBN-13: 978-1-939675-28-6
ISBN-10: 1939675286

Hoc est sigillum meum

April 1

Dear Mr. Firth,

ou're probably thinking, "What is this middle-aged green-loving long-haired horse-riding big-toothed woman doing, writing all these letters to me?" and "Why do so many of my craziest groupies come from the earnest middle of the United States?" and all sorts of other questions which, frankly, I don't blame you for, even if I am hoping some of your worst assumptions will prove unfounded by the end of this rather short book.

You see, these letters aren't really about you—they're about desire, and loss, and the ocean water reaching its cool, salty fingers up warm thighs and underneath clinging bathing suits. Well, that's what *some* of them are about. I suspect others will be about taking ourselves seriously or not, about the rooms we live in for a time and then inhabit, for other people, all our lives, even when we walk outside and into other, more surprising buildings. Given my own particular predilections, there will also likely be turtles, horizons, moss, gravel, dreams of flying, and kisses. Definitely kisses.

I may watch interviews with you and read up on your life as part of my research, and I may not. I actually know very little about you, except that you seem to have—as someone once said to me—something that feels rare these days, a kindness. I think it's those brown eyes. And I read that you have, like me, struggled with depression, that you own up to those moments so many of us have where we look up at the moon and just can't figure out what the fuck we're standing here for; and that you love to read, which makes you a good person to any writer. Honestly, I'm not always sure you're real; but then, I'm not always sure I am, either.

So what am I doing, writing all these letters to you?

I have no idea.

Sincerely,

Ms. Katherine Riegel

April 2

Dear Colin,

Last night I dreamt about Patrick Stewart, which was surprising, considering just yesterday I decided to devote this month to you. At least he's British too, and yes, he was a crush of mine before you. There were pieces of mirror on the floor in his apartment and I wanted to vacuum them up but he said they were for an art project. He was both spiritual and strange, a kind of ghost, which I suppose is what most famous people are to the rest of us. Also I confess I write most about my dreams when my real life reads too much like VCR instructions, which you are (thankfully) old enough to remember.

I dream about you sometimes, but the one I can never forget was years ago and went like this:

You were driving a convertible with the top down,
in England because you were sitting on the right and
I was on the left, and you'd just told me you loved
me and I was so happy the whole world smelled like
lilacs—even your hand, that warm splay of twigs,
flowering in mine.

Yours,

Katie

April 3

Dear Mr. Firth,

I got to meet the poet Sharon Olds when I was in college, and though I already loved her poems, I loved her even more when she confessed to reading *People* magazine. I didn't read it and still don't—it always looked like printed commercials to me and I could never find a way to care about these lace-wing-thin slices of people's lives in which interviewers never ever asked, *How's your heart?*—but I saw, even at 19, what a gift this poet was giving us, telling us to ease up on ourselves, that to be human we would also be full of contradiction and colors.

I wonder what *People* magazine has had to say about you over the years? And is it easy for you to ignore whatever they say, to let all that go, to live in the secret revolutions of dark and light inside your own ribcage?

My writer friends joke that the AWP conference—where 15,000 writers gather once a year like a giant flock of birds of all species—is the one place a poet might know what it's like to be a celebrity. We all have our stories of accosting a favorite writer at the elevator, bursting with enthusiasm for the work she does or the last book he published but unable to do more than foam and stutter because even people of the word lose hold of language when hoping so hard for connection with mystery, or at least connection with someone who led them to mystery. Sharon Olds is that kind of celebrity now, with twelve books and a lifetime of poems making claims for the body. If I ran into her at AWP some time I don't know what I'd call her: Ms. Olds, Sharon, Beautiful Poet?

Just as I don't know whether to call you Mr. Firth, person whose mysteries I don't know and so must respect, or Colin, my maybe-friend, man with an accent that cracks open language and shows me its insides again, its pounding urgency, its spiderweb veins carrying meaning away from and back again to the source.

Your maybe-friend,

Katie R.

April 4

Dear Colin,

My lover from Yorkshire tells me I could call you "duck," a term of endearment in the quirky north. Actually I prefer "love," something I've heard in enough British movies to be comfortable with. Besides, it goes with my Buddhist ideals to think of people as love-the-noun, these bodies and minds fluorescing with every breath.

This morning I had milk in my tea instead of cream, missing that rich nuance even as I sipped happy from my favorite drink. I keep trying sugar substitutes to make my tea guilt-free, but I always go back: real sugar, half-and-half. I want my pleasures unadulterated, like running down a hill at full speed, no hesitating, no slowing down, hurtling all out with the air filling and refilling my lung-sails til I come to the bottom, temporarily empty, where I may choose to climb up again or lie down in the cradling grass and search the sky for all the clouds I can see in the shape of ducks.

TTFN,

Katie

April 5

Dear Mr. Firth,

I apologize. In that last letter I intended to ask after *your* tea preferences. I fell asleep last night imagining your mornings:

you swim up towards the surface of waking life slowly, knowing everything will be different after you break through and breathe. You are as slow moving as a manatee; you reach for your wife's shoulder and together you pull yourselves onto the shore. Sometimes in the distance you hear bells and you hope they are not low and solemn, not today, because then you would have to decide whether to ask your beloved if she hears them too, to decide whether you want to tell her the darkness is coming in again.

I know those mornings.

But let us banish them here, in this luminous, forever place. Here, the bells jingle and sing like windchimes, like sun over the grass, caught in the throats

of birds who wake each day—unlike you and me—
to the certainty of flight.

Like (a boy once signed a birthday card to me "like,
Mark" so as to avoid any possible misunderstand-
ing),

Katie

April 6

Dear Colin,

I t's not an excuse or even a reason—I admit I'm
writing to you mostly on a whim—but my life is
complicated at the moment. I'm on leave from my
job and my marriage, staying at my sister's horse
farm in the part of central Illinois where I grew up,
where I grew like grass and wind and the shadows
of clouds high up in the summer-blue sky.

And while some things are settled, it's still daunting
to think I will be returning to Florida next month,
to the tar pit of grief that is the town where my job
and my sweet soon-to-be-ex-husband live. To the
chance to cut and sew a new friendship from what
was a too-tight suit for both of us. From the land-
scape that is family that is sky that is horses that was
refuge when I needed it most.

Is it even fair to say the other complication, the ex-
istence of a lover who is neither here nor there, a
lover who thrilled my Anglophile heart with his English accent and how he spent his teen years riding

horses across the moors? Is it fair that his mother knew James Herriot, whose books we read aloud to each other in my 1970s childhood, my mother and sister and I? Is it fair that this lover and I don't know yet how to be together and still live in the world we cannot ignore, the world we created for ourselves in the years before we met?

Ah, the churlish and droning details. What's simple: I am between. It is a thousand miles from where I live now to where I must return.

But isn't that how things are for most of us?

Your uncertain friend,

Katie

April 7

Dear Colin,

Sometimes I forget how hard it is to write anything when I'm worrying about money. Because of
meditation, I can go whole days—more, even—
without worrying about money, which is far longer,
I suspect, than my father ever managed. Money
and its acorning away for the future drove his mind
nearly all his adult life, so that when he went off a
cliff, so to speak—his mind having suffered from
too much simultaneous gas and brake pedal action
for far too long—and had what we used to call a
breakdown, he was convinced the men building a
house next door were going to hold him hostage
and demand all his IRAs.

I wish this memory could smooth the crease from
between my black eyebrows and lead me back to the
kingdom of the moment inhabited so effortlessly by
my dogs snoring on their beds on the unvacuumed
floor. My father is gone somewhere now I hope he
never has to worry about money again.

Meanwhile I swallow car payments and rent like caterpillars and drive to the grocery store where lottery tickets hover and bob under the influence of millions of imagined wings.

Sincerely,

Katie

April 8

Dear Mr. Firth,

I went into town—that's 25 minutes drive from my sister's therapeutic horseback riding center to the nearest real grocery store—today and FORGOT TO BUY A GODDAMNED LOTTERY TICKET. I got my allergy medicine, bread, peanut butter, oranges, real cream for my tea, and my favorite chocolate eggs that you can only get right before Easter, but I forgot that three-inch square of hope. And I really want those millions for my sister, for the horses, for the autistic kids who come out and get to control something so much bigger than they are for a half hour at a time.

I could say I was distracted by the gold afternoon Illinois sun, or the thought of eight horses waiting for me to get home and dole out sweet flakes of hay.

But I really think time rearranged itself, as I am sure it often does, and at the crucial moment I was already crying because my lover did not believe how large and rare his heart is, after someone he once loved told him, again, that terrible lie. You know that lie, don't you? The one that makes you a mouse at the feast: uninvited, vermin, tiny, yet somehow responsible for ruining the whole thing.

Helplessly,

Katie

April 9

Dear Colin,

According to the internet, today is International Gin & Tonic Day, and that's exciting because gin's been my drink for twenty years. I didn't even know it was a British spirit when I first started drinking it, just that it tasted like pine trees. Two make me smile like a siren, three and everyone gets a hug.

I think, now, that gin also tastes like Rudyard Kipling, whose books and stories and poems my grandmother read to me when I was a child. She drank cocktails too, though I think bourbon was her choice; I only remember my mother making sure we had the right ingredients whenever her mother came to visit. I don't know what my grandmother was like when she was tipsy, because as a child I never thought about altered states, didn't drink alcohol until I was sixteen.

What I knew: She was fierce. She loved books. She argued politics with her friends, but my parents refused to argue. She taught me gin rummy, and another card game called spite & malice, and when she came to our house she was allowed to drink inside but had to smoke outside. It's her—Dot, she was called—I think of when sipping my fancy gin and tonic with extra lime, Dot's voice curled up in the hollow of my throat, unapologetic, entitled to both white gloves and flapper skirts, entitled to the world's respect, and ready to demand it with an impeccably polite clearing of the throat that sounds just a bit like a growl.

Cheers,

Katie

April 10

Dear Colin,

I'm thinking you probably have never read Robert Frost, who is sort of our version of William Wordsworth but considerably less enthralled, sometimes almost as bitter as a New England winter—and yes, I do realize how odd "New England" sounds when addressing a Brit. I wonder how I'd feel if I ever heard of a place named New Illinois? Bewildered, I'm thinking, because even here most people consider where I come from as bland as oatmeal. Even I keep leaving it.

But sometimes Illinois puts on its best April weather and you spend a day carrying hay out to the pasture and walking wooden paths over shallow water where turtles already sunbathe, muskrats swim, geese and ducks compare nesting sites and even a pair of swans poses in a nearby inlet.

Sometimes you just sit for an hour in the sun while great blue herons come and go from their rookery.

That's when you drive home crying and thinking of Robert Frost, who wrote about "inner weather" in one of his many poems that seems at first like a light pastoral but turns out to really speak of losing, of lostness. That's when it occurs to you that no leaving or returning is ever without the painful pushes and pulls of love.

Your in-between friend,

Katie

April 11

Dear Colin,

So a train engineer sees a semi-truck stopped on the tracks, it's a big silver cylinder of gasoline, and he barrels towards it, helpless, already feeling the fireball—

and opens his eyes to the windows covered in milk. It was a milk truck. How does this guy feel when he watches his son lift a glass of that white liquid and gulp? How does he feel about cows? It's awful but also funny, and has nothing to do with you except it's a true story I heard today and my first thought was of England and trains, how I envy other countries for their public transportation even as I suspect I would want to go places in England that only a car would take me, if I ever get there.

Oh it's on my bucket list, Anglophile that I am. High tea. Scones with clotted cream. Stonehenge. The Lake District. The moors. The England of my mind is the setting for so much of the life I've lived in books, which means nothing really bad can ever happen there—the tanker truck always turns out to be filled with harmless milk, the gun really a flashlight, the knife a goose feather cutting through the air to glide along my clavicle soft as a kiss.

Yours on the wrong continent,

Katie

April 12

Dear Mr. Firth,

Do famous people think more about their legacies than the rest of us? I know fame is both relative and transient, but aren't we all a bit obsessed with that game? *What will people say about me when I'm gone?* I want them to say, *It smelled of gardenias wherever she went. I sang once, because of her. She knew about birds, and that was useful.*

What I fear they will say: *She couldn't save them.*

Infamously,

Ms. R.

April 13

Dear Colin,

Today the little midges clustered in the air over the pasture, celebrating the return of warmth. Huge, fat houseflies buzzed in the house, pests we accidentally helped overwinter. And I find I cannot be sorry for the life of any winged thing, even the biting horseflies I know will come this summer and torture those great hoofed creatures I love. I could see what every flying creature does to me as torture, not taking my body along through the waves and currents of the air. Or I could watch the mosquito lift off from my arm, carrying with it the tiny ruby cells of my blood.

Always wishing for flight,

Katie

April 14

Dear Colin,

Are chilblains still common in England? Yesterday I wrote about the return of summer insects and today we had snow. And years ago when my mother went to England with her friend in April there wasn't much heat at the B&Bs where they stayed, which made socks knitted with good English wool more necessity than keepsake.

There is something especially awful about not being able to get warm, which may be why my showers are never short, despite any intentions. The hot water beats on the back of my neck and my skin becomes erect with goose bumps.

These are the questions we don't ask each other enough: do you like long or short showers? Would you rather be too hot or too cold? What is your favorite invention that we almost never use anymore?

When I was small and went out to throw snowballs and sled in January, my mother put plastic bags over my socks before I slid my feet into my boots.

Shiveringly,

Katie

April 15

Dear Colin,

Today is tax day in the United States. I think I will turn on the electric blanket and lower the blinds and forget all politics and let the sun go out behind the just-budding trees and climb into bed and wait for my love to come home and kiss the pink parts of me that will never add up on any form.

Warmly,

Katie

April 16

Dear Colin,

Corresponding is like walking a dirt path through the forest and knowing there will be others on that same path getting mud on their sneakers or whistling or stubbing toes on arthritic roots. Maybe we're not walking side by side, mingling sweat when our arms touch, but we're walking through the ghosts of each other and hearing the same birds.

There are parts of me only kept alive through the words of others, like the flickering belief that I might be beautiful, this pale, overfull body capable of inciting fingertips to want more, to slide under and in, while someone's mouth says *yes* and *love* and *together*.

What do you need kept alive, what do you need touched gentle inside so you can bloom again?

Your friend,

Katie

April 17

Dear Colin,

The clouds are solidly annoying and the wind doesn't know anything—I think they both dropped out of high school in that terrible period where they still thought spitwads were funny and *everyone* was lame. Maybe they just want attention like psychologists say about troubled teens, they're acting out by making the middle of April miserable in that "maybe I need my earmuffs again" way.

I know we all want attention—if I could I'd still be doing splits and back bends and fluttering my long eyelashes to get adults to notice me—but there are ways and ways, right? I'll stop and lean down for hyacinths with their showy smell, ladybugs trundling red through the grass.

Me, these days I'm as shameless as a god and as directive: I'm distributing flyers, wearing my own face on a t-shirt, carrying a big sign with an arrow pointing down saying *Love me*.

Love,

Me

April 18

Dear Colin,

When you go out to the pasture and the horse lying flat on the ground in the sun doesn't even lift her head but looks lazily at you from her brown eye, do you panic? Or do you put the halter on anyway and coax her up like a sleepy teenager, promising a walk down between the not-yet-planted cornfields, a few minutes to stuff as much spring grass into her mouth as she can? And when she stops stock-still and stretches out to a natural show-horse stance because she's never been on this side of the fence and the big rock could be anything, could be a threat to run from or stomp with her hooves, what do you whisper to those forward-pointed ears, to the beast thrumming with tension—

do you lie and say there's nothing to worry about, ever, my beauty, my palomino love?

From the prairie,

Katie

April 19

Dear Colin,

One afternoon when we were kids my brother was thirsty, so he lifted the old pump handle but instead of water wasps came out. This is not a metaphor, though it could be. Only for most people this happens not once but again and again, and the best we can hope for is not to learn that every possible good thing could come out stinging but to keep admitting our thirst and to open our mouths anyway.

To hope,

Katie

April 20

Dear Colin,

Today I had to drive away from my lover. We took a shower together and cried, because it would be a month before we saw each other again. Don't believe technology really makes it just like you're with someone because you can see him on a screen. Try telling that to a cat or dog. Writing letters used to make me feel less lonely, their solidity, the same material I could make airplanes out of.

No. Today I believe what a dog believes: only what I can smell is real. I need something in my hands. I may go digging in the back yard, searching for fresh scents.

I think you know what it is to leave,

Katie

April 21

Dear Colin,

Listen to me, sifting through the window like
ash. I'm the fallout from some huge explosive ca-
tastrophe. We all are. We're carbon: diamond, bone,
burning. Every day I get older and for some reason
the world doesn't panic. I'm a grizzly bear standing
on my hind legs mistaken for Bigfoot. I'm a sundog,
a mini-rainbow, winking down at you in your curly
brown hair. I'm the dry boots someone is holding
above her head while she wades the river. There's
going to be an other side. You'd better fucking believe it.

To the other side,

Katie

April 22

Dear Colin,

*S*ome days every news story I read wounds me, bruising my interior organs and sunburning my skin til I can't even move my eyes without hurting. What makes those days—this day—so vulnerable? Is it because of the rain yesterday, our mother's ashes washed away from where my sister and I finally scattered them by the river, five years late? But there is always rain, there are always ashes. When the Vikings first came, Alcuin of York wrote, *Never before has such a terror appeared in Britain…nor was it thought an inroad from the sea could be made.*

But isn't it always nearly disaster? Ice sheets advancing or retreating, cruelty as impossible to stand against as the waves. I don't expect my feet to stay solid in the swirling sand. What I want to know is this: whether to slog back to the dubious beach or fall forward into the crushing arms of the sea.

Yours in disaster,

Katie

April 23

Dear Colin,

No one told us adulthood was just an extended stay in the neighbor's treehouse, with no dinner bell ringing to call us home where someone else would make us wash our hands, sit down to eat, and clear the table afterwards. No, we're just kneeling on a plank floor with a lantern while the world grows bigger and darker outside. In the morning, perhaps, we'll take stock, catalogue what we have and what we need. Then we'll pull back the hatch and peer towards the ground, unsure how much time passed—forty years, already?—while the stars wheeled around us and we dreamed our lives were old photo albums, images captured and chronicled as if important.

To childhood,

Katie

April 24

Dear Colin,

I dreamt my ex-husband and his girlfriend were ghosts. Only some people could see them, interact with them, and didn't mind. Their life together went on, semi-visible. It wasn't until my lover and I fell into the sea that I realized we were ghosts too. We couldn't drown. My arms were paper but I could breathe.

Is that what happens when a marriage ends? Everyone dies but we go on anyway: disappearing, reappearing, falling. Our arms too heavy to keep up the old struggle, our new selves less delicate than we thought.

From the afterlife,

Katie

April 25

Dear Colin,

I joke that I'm allowed to be moody because I'm a poet. It's part of the job description, along with flowing hair (check) and a penchant for wearing all black (I often fail on that one, I confess—I like green too much).

But it's fucking exhausting, shivering back from full-Florida-sun-smile to ice-bath-tears, all because someone answered tersely or gave away something you would have loved to have or you wandered too long in the home improvement store and when you finally asked for help no one tried to even understand what you needed. It's just when that happens the floor feels unsteady and your own front door looks unfamiliar and soon you're wondering if you stepped into the wrong life.

I swear I said these words on the phone to my long-suffering engineer lover just this afternoon, "I feel happy now." I swear I said that. I understand why people get words tattooed on their skin.

You never really know someplace until you've been there. Today at 1:42pm, I was there. Wherever happy is.

To that place,

Katie

April 26

Dear Colin,

*S*ay your car breaks down on a country road thirty miles from the nearest mechanic. Say you have a rat in the kitchen, clumsy enough to make noise at night. Say your dinner out with friends turns out to be you, alone, at a table with two couples talking about TV shows you have never seen and don't want to. Say you're going to sign papers to sell your house at a loss of thousands, the house you bought with your not-anymore-husband. Say you keep thinking that if you only fell to your knees on sharp gravel, let your blood drip down between the stones, you could save everyone you love—or at least feel you'd done everything possible, everything you could. Say the world never asks you to do anything so simple.

The end of the month approaches,

Katie

April 27

Dear Colin,

I had another dream about you! We were at a party, and we wanted so desperately just to talk to each other, to talk like new friends who disregard time and hunger and tact, to talk like old friends who linger over a meal and encourage each other to have just one more biscuit. But we kept getting interrupted, people stopping by to chat, the drinks in their hands buzzing with need—

and would you believe it? This letter just got interrupted by a workman at the door, coming to fix the cold-water shower handle that won't turn. If I were Coleridge and I could claim genius, I might say the words that were lost because of him would have changed everything, perhaps even brought about paradise.

But all I really want is to go back to that dream, find a quiet corner and a couple of comfortable chairs, and talk with you. In the dream, you see, I wasn't self-conscious about your fame or my cheap clothes. I wasn't riding in the back of our 1970s blue Dodge station wagon, youngest, with the least right to be heard. In the dream, we would have talked about how everything comes back to childhood, our adult lives just lures on the end of a fishing line, thrown out into the rushing water and then reeled back, every time.

To dream conversations,

Katie

April 28

Dear Colin,

Another word for *waiting* is *no-land*. Another word for *lost* is *water*. When moving across the vast distances we have here in the States, we cannot help but talk at length with the sky. Inside every morning is a rabbit, crouched and ready to run. I am leaving my homeland to go back to the sun and sea. I have said this before but no matter where I go I am always leaving.

To the road,

Katie

April 29

Dear Colin,

I imagine you reading this letter to your wife. I imagine she reminds you what you aren't: a statue, a moth, glass, someone else's reason. I imagine you want to curl up into the beauty of the inside of her elbow, to be so clever you make her laugh with her whole body.

I am not always self-absorbed.

In an interview you said nothing had ever happened to you. But the world happens to us every moment—the bed happens exactly as you lie down on it, the cat with its eyes closed in the sun is happening perfectly when you see it, the doubt happens slimy in your throat at the worst time (because every time is the worst).

You were being humble. I am not trying to contradict you. I only want to say that it matters, this moment with the window closed, keeping you in.

Your friend, truly,

Katie

April 30

Dear Colin,

I AM COMING TO ENGLAND! This summer, just for a visit, to see my Brit's family and the hills of Yorkshire. I thought I should tell you, although I have no hopes of meeting you. In fact my plans involve discovering just how naked my lover can get me during walks on the moors. I am getting old enough now to be amused by young people and their assumptions about the propriety of the middle-aged. If I were to be caught with the goose bumps covering my bare white flesh and my head thrown back in concentration on my own pleasure, the man I love reminding me what my skin is really for—well, it wouldn't be a kiss from you but I'd brag anyway about that time I made love in England and it was so beautiful the whole country cried fresh tears everyone else thought were just the usual afternoon drops of rain.

To the next chapter,

Katie

Acknowledgments

I am grateful to the editors of the Dead Letter Office at *The Offing*, who published five of these letters; and to the editors of *Hotel Amerika*, who will publish four of these letters in their 2016 issue.

Special thanks to Nicole Oquendo, who selected my chapbook as the winner of the Sundress Publications Chapbook Competition, giving the lie to my claim that I never win anything, and to Sundress Publications, for being open to writing that's in-between.

.

Printed in Great Britain
by Amazon